LET IT
GO!

Breaking Free from Fear and Anxiety

Tony Evans

MOODY PUBLISHERS
CHICAGO

All Scripture quotations, unless otherwise indicated, are taken from the *New
American Standard Bible®*, Copyright © The Lockman Foundation 1960, 1962,
1963, 1968, 1971, 1972, 1973, 1975, 1977, 1995. Used by permission.

Scripture quotations marked NIV are taken from the *Holy Bible, New International Version®*. NIV®. Copyright © 1973, 1978, 1984 by International
Bible Society. Used by permission of Zondervan Publishing House. All
rights reserved.

Library of Congress Cataloging-in-Publication Data

Evans, Anthony T.
     Let it go! : breaking free from fear and anxiety / Tony Evans.
       p. cm.
     ISBN-10: 0-8024-4378-8
     ISBN-13: 978-0-8024-4378-6
     1. Anxiety—Religious aspects—Christianity. 2. Fear—Religious
aspects—Christianity. I. Title.

BV4908.5.E93 2005
248.8'6—dc22

                                                                    2005017671

We hope you enjoy this book from Moody Publishers. Our goal is to provide high-quality, thought-provoking books and products that connect
truth to your real needs and challenges. For more information on other
books and products written and produced from a biblical perspective, go to
www.moodypublishers.com or write to:

Moody Publishers
820 N. LaSalle Boulevard
Chicago, IL 60610

5 7 9 10 8 6

Printed in the United States of America

CONTENTS

1

Breaking Free

FROM

Emotional Strongholds

Perhaps you have heard the story of the man who was hiking alone in the mountains when he slipped and fell off a cliff. The only thing that kept him from plunging to his death down a deep gorge was a tree growing from the side of the cliff. As he fell, the hiker grabbed a limb and hung on for dear life.

Clinging tightly to the tree limb, the man began shouting desperately, hoping that someone might be coming along the trail behind him. "Help! Help! Is there anyone up there?" But no answer came back.

Finally, as he neared exhaustion, and his grip on the tree limb began to weaken, the hiker yelled again in total desperation, "Is there anyone up there?"

This time, a booming voice answered, "Yes, I'm here."

The hiker was elated. "This is great! Who are you?"

"It's the Lord."

"Oh, thank You, Lord!" the hiker gasped. "What do you want me to do?"

"Let go, and I'll catch you."

But the terrified hiker was too afraid to let go of the limb. So he cried out again, "Is there anyone up there?"

The Lord answered again, "I said, let go of the limb, and I'll save you."

But the hiker couldn't bring himself to let go of the only piece of security he thought he had. So after thinking about it for a minute, he shouted, "Is there anyone *else* up there?"

That fictional hiker is like a lot of real-life Christians who are clinging desperately to all manner of emotional security blankets. These believers often think their twisted-up emotions are their source of security, when in fact, these emotional problems are the very things keeping them from being really free.

What Christians in this situation need to do is what the hiker in our story needed to do: Let go of that which cannot rescue them anyway and trust God to honor His promises.

My goal for this booklet is to help people in bondage to various emotions and anxieties break free through the truth of God's Word and the power of the Holy Spirit. We'll address the anxiety first, and then I want to give you biblical examples and patterns for handling the emotional storms of life that are sure to come your way.

The word I will be using for these traps (into which even Christians can fall) is *stronghold*. My prayer is that Christians in these predicaments will learn to understand and apply the Bible to their lives in ways that they can let go of any emotional stronghold the Enemy may have built in their lives.

Freedom Is Available

If you or someone you care about is in the grip of an emotional stronghold such as anger, depression, fear, worry—or even some sort of substance abuse—I am here to tell you that there is freedom available in Jesus Christ.

The world's word for things that hold people hostage is *addiction*. We hear it said that people are addicted to drugs, alcohol, sex, or whatever it may be. The problem I have with this word is the implication it often has that we are powerless victims of our circumstances.

In other words, calling something an addiction suggests that we have an excuse for what we're doing, either because we don't have the ability to break it, someone else caused it and thus it isn't our fault, or we have bad genes or a bad environment that set us up for this problem. Some people may even say their addiction has all of these elements.

Now I know that many psychologists, psychiatrists, and other mental health professionals would argue that the concept of addiction doesn't mean there is no way out. But for our purposes in this booklet, I'm not interested in what the professionals say nearly as much as I am in the popular perception of what it means to have an addiction—for two reasons.

The first reason is that I believe the average person thinks of an addiction as something that is somehow not the victim's responsibility, which often helps the person dodge the real issue. The second reason is that calling something an addiction doesn't address the spiritual dimension of the problem, which is needed to find the answer.

The word *stronghold* takes us to the real issue because it takes us to our spiritual makeup and to the Word of God. When we get the spiritual part of the equation fixed, the emotional and the physical parts will begin to fall in line.

THE ENEMY'S STRONGHOLDS

The *New International Version* of the Bible says, "The weapons we fight with are not the weapons of the world. On the contrary, they have divine power to demolish strongholds" (2 Corinthians 10:4). A stronghold is like a fortress the Enemy has built on your turf, which is why the *New American Standard Bible* translates this word as "fortresses."

Our Enemy, of course, is Satan, who can build strongholds in our minds and hearts if we allow him to gain a foothold in our lives. The Devil is a relentless

Enemy who is not content just to conquer territory in your life. He wants to erect strongholds, which he can then use as his base of operations to attack you whenever he feels like it. When you have an enemy who can take refuge in his stronghold and come out from it to attack you at will, you won't get anywhere until you tear down that stronghold and leave the Enemy with no place to hide.

Our emotions are particularly vulnerable to satanic attack because emotions are feelings that have no intellect of their own. An emotion is a deep-down, often immediate and intense, reaction to something that happens to us. That's why we talk about our gut-level feelings, for example, or say of someone who has upset us, "He really burns me up."

People who are in emotional strongholds usually know something is wrong. When they get up they don't say, "Good morning, Lord," but "Good Lord, it's morning!" In severe cases these people may feel as if they are struggling just to survive because they feel hopeless and can't seem to shake the emotional traps they're in.

Emotional strongholds are attitudes that result in actions that hold a person hostage to something contrary to the will of God. God never ordained for His children to go to bed and wake up depressed every day of their lives. All of us have times when we struggle with our emotions because we are imperfect people living in a fallen world. But strongholds are feelings or actions that dominate your life and consume most of your time and effort.

For many Christians, the cause of their emotional trauma is not the emotions themselves. It is because they have not understood their true identity in Christ or learned to live by grace—so they don't know how to respond to the spiritual causes of their attitudinal distresses.

THREE WRONG WAYS TO DEAL WITH
EMOTIONAL STRONGHOLDS

A person who is in emotional distress but doesn't look for the spiritual root of the problem is like someone who turns off the smoke alarm in his house and opens the windows to let the smoke out without ever looking for the fire.

As you know, those are wrong ways to deal with a house fire because all they do is mask the symptoms instead of solving the problem. In the same way, many people use the wrong methods to deal with emotional strongholds because they fail to understand their true nature. I see at least three ways that people try to deal with the pain of an emotional problem without really confronting it.

The first of these is through outright denial, which could be called suppression. This is when a person knows something is wrong but makes a conscious and deliberate effort to run from or bury the problem. People in this situation may constantly insist they are fine and everything is cool when they know that's not true.

A second faulty way to deal with emotional strongholds is through repression, or unconscious denial. This is where the pain may be so intense that the person has pushed it deep down below the level of consciousness. These people may no longer be aware of why they feel the way they feel or do the things they do. Someone's denial may be conscious at first, but if it goes on long enough, the person may actually succeed in pushing the problem out of consciousness.

A third wrong way to deal with such problems is to bury them with busyness, drown them in alcohol, or try to drug them out of existence. Those in this category who don't fall into substance abuse may stay on the go constantly, or always make sure that either the television or some other noise is going at all times—so they don't have to hear the alarm going off in their souls.

> PAINFUL EMOTIONS ARE LIKE THE PAIN SIGNALS OUR BODIES SEND OUT TO ALERT US THAT SOMETHING IS WRONG.

Remember when you were a child and you didn't want to hear what your brother or sister was saying? You would put your hands over your ears and shout, "I can't hear you!" or start singing to drown them out. That's fine for kids, but it's a terrible way to live as an adult.

Painful emotions are like the pain signals our bodies send out to alert us that something is wrong. You can ignore or deny pain, but if there is something really wrong it will not just go away. Just as when we are in physical pain and need to go to the doctor to find out why, when we are hurting emotionally we need to find out why.

Please don't misunderstand what I said about the fields of psychology and psychiatry. When practiced correctly—that is, biblically—the mental health disciplines can help people discover and correct what is wrong. But when there is a failure to take the spiritual side of an issue into account, or to see that emotional problems have spiritual roots, then only the symptoms are being addressed.

THE CAUSE OF EMOTIONAL STRONGHOLDS

Emotional strongholds are fortresses the Enemy has built in our minds and hearts. They are built on his lies about who we are and what has happened to us or what we have done. This means that the root cause of these problems has a lot to do with the Enemy's specialty, which is either trying to lead us into sin or ensnaring us in our own sin or someone else's sin until we are completely bound up.

I don't want to deny or dismiss the fact that some emotional problems have physiological ties. There is a strong link between the physical and emotional parts of our makeup, because we are whole beings and are not made up of separate compartments. For example, if you are told you have cancer and you react with fear, that fear has a basis in fact. Feeling fear in the face of cancer is a normal reaction, not a stronghold.

But the kind of bondage the Bible calls a stronghold is rooted either in our own sin, in the sin of someone else, or in the fact that we live in a sin-tainted environment. You may have been abused as a child, and as a result of the abuser's sin against you, you are in emotional bondage as an adult.

Now you may be dealing with this in sinful ways with drugs or alcohol, or by taking out your anger on someone else. But in any case, the root cause of emotional strongholds is sin—which is why any solution that doesn't address the spiritual issue is not really a solution.

The Bible reveals that the entry of negative emotions into the human race was because of sin. God put Adam and Eve in a perfect environment, but as we see in Genesis chapter 3, Satan came onto the scene and enticed first Eve, and then Adam, to rebel against God. The first thing that happened after they ate the forbidden fruit was, "The eyes of both of them were opened, and they knew that they were naked; and they sewed fig leaves together and made themselves loin coverings" (3:7).

Before this, Adam and Eve had been naked but without shame (Genesis 2:25). But now they were ashamed of their nakedness and had to cover themselves. The emotion of shame entered into the human race. There was also fear, for in Genesis 3:9–10 we read that Adam and Eve hid when they heard the sound of God walking in the garden. "Then the Lord God called to the man, and said to him, 'Where are you?' He said, 'I heard the sound of You in the garden, and I was afraid because I was naked; so I hid myself.'"

And it gets worse. The murder of Abel by Cain involved the emotions of jealousy, anger, and hatred on Cain's part because God accepted his brother's offering while rejecting his. It's interesting that Cain was also depressed. When Cain's bloodless sacrifice was rejected, "his countenance fell" (Genesis 4:5). But instead of dealing with his emotions by turning to God in repentance and faith, his anger drove him inwardly into depression and outwardly into murder. Depression is well described as anger turned inward.

There is quite a grocery list of powerful emotions and destructive patterns of behavior that entered the human race through sin. That's why a person who is trying to overcome a stronghold without looking to the spiritual reason for it will never find the source of the fire in his emotional house, so to speak. He will hear the shrill sound of the fire alarm, but his efforts will be geared toward silencing that alarm.

Now lest you doubt the causative connection between sin and emotional strongholds, look at what God said to Cain when He saw that Cain was angry and depressed. "Why are you angry? And why has your countenance fallen? If you do well, will not your countenance be lifted up? And if you do not do well, sin is crouching at the door; and its desire is for you, but you must master it" (Genesis 4:6–7).

This was probably the first counseling session in history, and God the Counselor went straight to the heart of the problem! Sin wanted to master Cain by holding him in bondage to his wrong thoughts and the resulting wrong emotions.

THREE CATEGORIES OF EMOTIONAL STRONGHOLDS

Let me briefly mention three general categories of emotional strongholds, relating to where we are in our lives. The first category is those strongholds that are rooted in the pain of the past. This may be childhood abuse, as previously mentioned, or some other traumatic experience in your past that is impairing your ability to function today.

These experiences are like recordings in the mind that keep rewinding and playing every time something triggers the bad memory. Satan keeps his finger on the play button, and he's an expert at knowing what it takes to start that recording running again. He doesn't stop there either. He'll try to make sure that every time you replay that past trauma, it seems worse than the time before. He'll add to it until it seems as if your whole life is in bondage to the past.

Here's one other trick the Devil likes to play on you when you are being held bondage to the emotions of past traumas. He will bring people into your life who went through what you went through and have not been victorious over it—and soon you'll be caught up in their lack of victory because misery loves company.

A second category of strongholds is made up of problems in the present. What is going on in your life right now may be overwhelming you. If anybody could have been depressed and in bondage to his circumstances, it was the apostle Paul. He wrote about what he had endured for the gospel's sake:

> [I have been] beaten times without number, often in danger of death. Five times I received from the Jews thirty-nine lashes. Three times I was beaten with rods, once I was stoned, three times I was shipwrecked, a night and a day I have spent in the deep. I have been on frequent journeys, in dangers from rivers, dangers from robbers, dangers from my countrymen, dangers from the Gentiles, dangers in the city, dangers in the wilderness, dangers on the sea, dangers among false brethren; I have been in labor and hardship, through many sleepless nights, in hunger and thirst, often without food, in cold and exposure. Apart from such external things, there is the daily pressure on me of concern for all the churches. (2 Corinthians 11:23–28)

Few of us could put together a list of trials that could compare to this. But instead of throwing in the towel or hiding in a corner, Paul moved on because he had learned that his sufferings were the key to God's power within him. As he put it, "When I am weak, then I am strong" (2 Corinthians 12:10). We can hold to this truth in our struggles as well.

A third category of strongholds relates to the future. Many people are so afraid of what might happen that they don't want to get out of bed in the morning. As bad as it is to be held in bondage to the past or the present, it may even be crueler to be a prisoner to tomorrow, especially if our fear centers on a bunch of "what-ifs" that haven't even happened. What if I get cancer or have a heart attack? What if one of my children dies?

Jesus told us, "Do not worry about tomorrow" (Matthew 6:34). Fear of tomorrow is another emotional trap the Enemy has laid for us.

THE CURE FOR EMOTIONAL STRONGHOLDS

We've already seen that trying to deny or suppress painful emotions doesn't do any good, nor does it help to try and avoid them by keeping busy and never facing them. That doesn't work because Satan always has another thing around the corner to bring up the pain again.

So don't try to tell yourself there's nothing wrong when you know better. And don't listen to other people who are telling you just to snap out of it or get over it. I love the epitaph that a person who was considered the town hypochondriac had engraved on his tombstone: "I told you I was sick."

Emotions are real, but I want to emphasize something. Emotions have no intellect of their own. They have to borrow thoughts in order to emote off of them. Our emotions only respond to what we think. They are by-products of our thought lives. Therefore, whoever controls our thoughts determines how we feel.

If the Devil is controlling your thinking, you'll feel the way he wants you to feel. If God is controlling your thinking, you'll feel the way God wants you to feel. The reason is, as the Bible says, "As [a man] thinks within himself, so he is" (Proverbs 23:7). Your thinking is the key to overcoming emotional strongholds.

Jesus said, "You will know the truth, and the truth will make you free" (John 8:32). Notice that He said it is not enough just to hear the truth but to know it—to let the truth of God's Word settle down in your mind and begin to shape the way you think. When you do that, then you will be set free.

Satan and his demons are like cockroaches when the light comes on. They scatter because Satan can't handle the truth. He can handle you and your ideas, but when you come at this issue of strongholds from the perspective of what God says, you will experience a change in your thinking that will result in a change in your emotions.

Perhaps you have never come to grips with your true identity in Christ, that you are a "new creature" for whom "the old things passed away; behold, new things have come" (2 Corinthians 5:17). If you are still operating on the basis of your old identity in Adam, you are bound to feel the way the Devil wants you to feel because he controlled you when you were still in Adam—that is, still in your sins.

> YOU CANNOT DWELL ON BOTH THE THINGS OF GOD AND THE LIES OF SATAN.

Part of your new identity in Christ is the power He gives you to overcome any attack or lie of the Enemy. One of the foundational passages in this study is 2 Corinthians 10:4 (NIV): "The weapons we fight with are not the weapons of the world. On the contrary, they have divine power to demolish strongholds."

If we did not have the power as new creatures in Christ to demolish Satan's strongholds in our hearts and minds, then God would not command us to control our thinking, as He does in Philippians 4:8. Paul gave a list of things that are right and wholesome and godly, and then wrote, "Dwell on these things."

The human mind cannot entertain two contradictory thoughts at the same time. Therefore, you cannot dwell on both the things of God and the lies of Satan. One or the other will eventually win the battle for your mind. And the winner of this battle gains the ground on which to build either a tower of truth that protects you against Satan's attacks—or a stronghold that keeps you in bondage.

Now don't misunderstand. If you have been held captive in an emotional stronghold for any length of time, this thing is not going to fall all at once. Sure, there are times when God gives instantaneous deliverance, but those are the exceptions to the rule.

Most of the time, you take a stronghold apart brick by brick—by focusing your mind on Jesus Christ and developing an intimacy with Him that grows and grows until His thoughts are becoming your thoughts. And the way you do that is by saturating your mind with His Word, seeking Him in prayer and fasting, and obeying the truth as the Spirit reveals it to you.

A WORD OF ENCOURAGEMENT

Whatever it is that is causing you to feel the way you feel right now is never the last word. Whatever is going wrong in your life, as long as God is on His throne, He can give you the last word on your situation. When we treat our emotions as the final statement, we miss out on the truth of a great word that Jesus gave us in John 16:33. "In the world you have tribulation."

You say, "Tony, that's not encouraging news." Well, I'd be lying to you if I told you that you will never have any more trials and battles, or that the Enemy will leave you alone once you learn how to tear down his strongholds. But read on in John 16:33. Jesus said, "Take courage; I have overcome the world." This is the last word!

As we wrap up this first chapter of our study, I want

to mention the critical role of the church in helping believers overcome emotional strongholds. If you are fighting these things as a "lone ranger" Christian without connecting yourself to a local church, you are out of the will of God.

But more than that, trying to make it on your own is about as effective as one lone soldier facing an army. You can't do it alone, and you weren't designed to. You need the encouragement and the ministry of the church.

The church is the place to find people who will help you keep your eyes on the Lord when you can't see Him. The church may not be able to solve all your problems, but God's people can help you focus on Him so that you're not drowned by what you're going through.

2

BREAKING FREE
FROM
ANXIETY
STRONGHOLDS

Two friends were talking one day when one said to the other, "Man, you sure look worried."

"Yeah, I am," came the answer. "I've got so many problems that if something were to go wrong today, it would be at least two weeks before I could get around to worrying about it!"

My brother or sister in Christ, if you have so many things on your worry list that you're backed up two weeks, then you have far more worry in your life than God ever intended you to have. In fact, it's safe to say that anyone in this condition is being held in the grip of an anxiety stronghold.

Many people worry about anything and everything, and that's not limited to adults. Young people worry too, like the boy who prayed one night, "Now I lay me down to rest, I hope to pass tomorrow's test. And if I die before I wake, that's one less test I'll have to take."

I'm not talking about momentary worries, like a test in school, but an orientation to life that says, "I'm so afraid that something awful is going to happen, or that my life is going to fall apart that I can't function the way God wants me to function."

One reason anxiety is such a common problem is that it's available in so many varieties. We can worry about yesterday, today, tomorrow, jobs, money, health, children, what people will say or think, or even nuclear war and global warming. There is no lack of things to worry about.

ANXIETY COMES AT A HIGH COST

The signs of anxiety are all around us. The number of people taking prescription antianxiety or antidepressant medications is astronomical. Besides these, some people use alcohol and illegal drugs to calm their fears or escape reality. Others seek constant entertainment or even go shopping in an attempt to quiet their anxieties.

Chronic worriers often have physiological symptoms as well, including headaches, heart palpitations, sweat pouring down the forehead, and panic attacks.

We don't have to spend a lot of time proving that anxiety is a problem. What I want you to see is what God says about it, because that's where we will find the answers we need to break out of the Enemy's stronghold of anxiety.

You may already know where I'm headed. In a very famous part of the Sermon on the Mount, Jesus commanded us three times not to worry about the things of life (Matthew 6:25, 31, 34). The word Jesus used for worry in this passage refers to being strangled or choked. That's a perfect description of what a stronghold does to us. It gets a stranglehold that keeps us from breathing normally. We feel as if we're choking.

THE DIFFERENCE BETWEEN WORRY AND CONCERN

If Jesus Christ tells us not to do something, to do it is a sin. That's why I say worry is a sin. Now someone will say, "Oh, I'm not worried. I'm just concerned . . ."

Of course, there is a legitimate thing called concern for people, issues, and events that are important to us. The apostle Paul said concerning all that he had suffered, "Apart from such external things, there is the daily pressure on me of concern for all the churches" (2 Corinthians 11:28).

If a loved one is in the hospital, we are right to be concerned about that person's health. If you have a wayward child, I know you are concerned about that child's future. But concern is different than chronic, choking worry in at least two ways.

First, legitimate concern moves us to do all that we

can to address the situation, while worry paralyzes us. In the case of a sick family member, we can see that she has proper medical care, perhaps arrange for care when she gets home, and encourage her to change anything that may have contributed to the illness. There are any number of things that can be done to alleviate the concern.

> # WORRY IS INTEREST PAID ON TROUBLE BEFORE IT'S DUE.

Second, legitimate concern trusts God, while worry drives us toward panic and fear and away from God. When it comes to the things we can't do anything about, such as a wayward child's decision to go astray, we can commit these things to God and trust His love and wisdom.

Paul said he was concerned for the churches because he knew that false teachers were out to deceive God's people, as he told the elders of Ephesus (Acts 20:29–30). But instead of lying awake at night in anxiety or wringing his hands in despair, Paul continued to teach sound doctrine, disciple qualified leaders, warn the saints, and stay committed to God's purposes.

Worry is concern gone haywire. It becomes a problem when it owns you during the day and keeps you awake at night. Worry is interest paid on trouble before it's due. Anxiety is so serious that Jesus said it can even keep you from hearing the Word of God and growing by it (Luke 8:14). On one occasion when His friend Martha was running around trying to get a meal ready,

Jesus gently rebuked her: "Martha, Martha, you are worried and bothered about so many things" (Luke 10:41).

WORRY MEANS YOUR FOCUS IS OFF

Jesus began His teaching on worry in Matthew 6 by saying, "For this reason I say to you, do not be worried about your life" (v. 25). This takes us back to verse 24, where Jesus said you cannot serve two masters, God and money. If God is your Master, then He is also your Father, as Jesus went on to point out in the rest of the passage. And if God is your good and perfect Father, He will love you and care for you.

In other words, if you are being eaten up by excessive worry, your focus is not on your heavenly Father. You've got your eyes on the wrong authority.

Now money has a certain amount of authority in our world because it is the medium of exchange—and people with the most money are often in charge. But money does not have the power to deliver you from worry, even if you have a lot of it. The richest people are often those who worry about money the most. It's a myth and a lie of the Devil that if you have all the money you want or need, your worries will be over.

Notice how Jesus illustrated His point. "For this reason I say to you, do not be worried about your life, as to what you will eat or what you will drink; nor for your body, as to what you will put on. Is not life more than food, and the body more than clothing? Look at the birds of the air, that they do not sow, nor do they reap nor gather into barns, and yet your heavenly Father feeds them. Are you not worth much more than they?" (Matthew 6:25–26).

Jesus drew an example from nature, that of the birds. Don't read over verse 26 too fast, because what Jesus said there is important. He did not say the birds' Creator feeds them, but "your heavenly Father." The birds of the air eat because your Daddy feeds them.

So if God takes care of birds, what does this say about His care for us? And what are we implying about God's care when we worry whether He will bother to feed and clothe us? This is why I say worry is a sin. It's really an insult to God. When we worry, we show that we have forgotten who our Daddy is.

I know that many people grew up in homes where the father left and didn't come back—or wasn't there at all. I grew up with people who had no father and could not count on a father's care. They may have had glorious mothers, but they did not have a father who could be depended upon. But God is not that kind of Father.

I was blessed with a father who was always there for me. I hold my father in the highest esteem for his faithfulness and hard work. He always took care of our family. He had to work and be responsible because God has never promised just to rain down steak and potatoes on us without our having to do anything.

There's a difference between trusting God and presuming on His grace. Expecting God to care for you while you do nothing is presuming on Him. We need to be responsible, but we also need to be confident that when we do what God expects of us, He is going to provide for our ultimate needs.

WORRY IS FUTILE

Jesus went on to say in Matthew 6, "And who of you by being worried can add a single hour to his life?" (v. 27). This takes us from the wrong focus of worry to its utter futility.

Worry is like a rocking chair. It requires a lot of effort, but it doesn't get you anywhere. Worry has never changed anything, except maybe the quality of the worrier's health. Worry may take hours off your life, but it won't add one hour to it.

WORRY INDICATES A LACK OF FAITH

"And why are you worried about clothing? Observe how the lilies of the field grow; they do not toil nor do they spin, yet I say to you that not even Solomon in all his glory clothed himself like one of these. But if God so clothes the grass of the field, which is alive today and tomorrow is thrown into the furnace, will He not much more clothe you? You of little faith!" (vv. 28–30).

Jesus hit on the real issue at the end of verse 30 when He rebuked excessive worriers for their "little faith." To worry is to question God's integrity, which is the opposite of believing Him.

Let me put it a little more bluntly. To worry is to say, "God, You are lying when You promise to meet my needs. You must not really be a good Father because I don't think I can trust You to do what You said." Heart-palpitating anxiety and strong faith cannot coexist in the same heart for any length of time. One or the other is going to win out.

The incompatibility of worry and faith is really evident in Jesus' conclusion to His argument as to why we must stop worrying. "Do not worry then, saying, 'What will we eat?' or 'What will we drink?' or 'What will we wear for clothing?' For the Gentiles eagerly seek all these things; for your heavenly Father knows that you need all these things" (vv. 31–32).

The word *Gentiles* is another term for unbelievers. They break their necks trying to get ahead—and well they should, since they are not trusting a heavenly Father to provide for them. But it doesn't make sense for us as Christians to wear ourselves out trying to do it all when our Father has the universe at His disposal.

I mentioned my hardworking father, who was a stevedore on the docks in Baltimore. He would work overtime if he had to in order to feed us, but he did not have the universe at his disposal. My daddy's work loading and unloading ships was backbreaking, and there were also times when he would be out of work for weeks or even several months due to a union strike.

When that happened, Daddy would go fishing to get food. He caught herring, which is a fish with about a million bones in it. Dad caught herring in nets, so we are talking about hundreds of herring. He would bring them home and my mother would freeze them. We had herring and eggs, herring and bologna sandwiches, herring for dinner, and herring à la mode for dessert. Everything was herring.

Trying to pick all the bones out of those little fish must have damaged me psychologically as a child, because from that time on I have hated fish and never eat it if I don't have to. But my point is that my earthly father was a good and faithful provider. He just didn't have anywhere near the resources of my heavenly Father. Daddy had to fish when the herring were running, but my heavenly Daddy created the fish that swam into my earthly daddy's net.

I never worried that my father would not take care of me, even when he was out of work. Jesus is saying that when we let worry and anxiety dominate us, we are showing a lack of faith in God's ability and desire to provide.

YOU CAN BREAK FREE
OF ANXIETY STRONGHOLDS

Are you ready to learn how to tear down that stronghold of anxiety the Enemy has built in your heart and mind? Jesus gave us the answer: We need to change priorities.

You may have memorized Matthew 6:33. Instead of worrying, Jesus said, "Seek first His kingdom and His righteousness, and all these things will be added to you." In other words, if you will spend your time and energy getting on board with what God is doing in the world, He has your back in terms of the other stuff of life.

Jesus then concluded with this statement, including His third command not to worry: "So do not worry about tomorrow; for tomorrow will care for itself. Each day has enough trouble of its own" (v. 34).

God gives you grace one day at a time. He will not give you tomorrow's grace today, and you don't need it. Why? "His compassions never fail. They are new every morning; great is Your faithfulness" (Lamentations 3:22–23). So if you are worried about what's going to happen tomorrow, you have missed the point. To worry about tomorrow is to lose your joy today.

You may say, "Tony, you don't know what I have to face tomorrow." No, I don't, but I can tell you that when tomorrow comes, God's grace will be sufficient for you. So should you stay up all night worrying about something? There's no need, because your Daddy in heaven is staying up to look after it.

In fact, whatever it is that has you bound up in anxiety only got to you in the first place after passing your Father's review. So even though it may not seem like it right now, He will not send you more than you can bear, as He promised in 1 Corinthians 10:13. People may wonder at times what kind of a God we are dealing with here. Well, Jesus told us. We are dealing with a God whose name is Daddy, who owns the world, and cares even for birds and flowers. Once you get that straight, everything else starts to fall into line.

WORRY IS A SIGNAL TO PRAY

What do you do when anxiety rears its ugly head and begins to twist a band of worry tightly around your mind and won't let go? The Bible says that the best antidote to worry is prayer.

Now I know someone is going to object that this is too simplistic an answer. Someone will say, "I've heard that all my Christian life. I'm carrying a real heavy burden and dying with worry, and you are telling me just to pray about it?"

WHOEVER OR WHATEVER CONTROLS OUR MINDS CONTROLS US.

Yes, I am. But lest you think prayer is too easy an answer, I am not talking about some two-minute exercise we go through where we simply repeat whatever the adult version is of the child's prayer, "God bless Mommy, God bless Daddy, God bless Grandma and Grandpa," and so forth.

I am talking about the kind of fervent, intense, forget-to-eat-or-deliberately-fast prayer in which, like Jacob (Genesis 32:24–32), you wrestle with God and refuse to let go until He blesses you. If you're carrying a heavy burden, pour out your heart to God. Nothing I am saying is intended to imply that no matter what your concerns are, all you have to do is just whistle a happy tune and pretend everything is fine.

WORRY ABOUT NOTHING; PRAY ABOUT EVERYTHING

To show you what is involved in prayer, and what prayer can do for a worrier, I want to go to Philippians 4:6–7. It says in verse 6, "Be anxious for nothing, but in everything by prayer and supplication with thanksgiving let your requests be made known to God."

When worry rears its ugly head, the first thing you need is not a pill to calm you down. Instead, God says we must make a shift in our focus, because whoever or whatever controls our minds controls us. Instead of focusing on and being controlled by worry, God wants us to focus on Him and allow His Word and Spirit to control us. That's why prayer is so important.

The formula here is simple. Worry about nothing, but pray about everything. The general word for *prayer* is used in Philippians 4:6, and the word *supplication* refers to asking for the answer to a specific need. So we have the general and specific, which is another way of saying we ought to pray about everything.

Some Christian homes used to have a framed motto on the wall that said, "Why worry when you can pray?" That's the right idea . . . though I think it should read, "You can't worry and pray."

PRAYING WITH THANKSGIVING BRINGS HOPE

But notice the wrinkle, if you will, that the Holy Spirit threw into Philippians 4:6. We are to pray "with thanksgiving." Gratitude is not only entirely fitting for the people of God, but it breeds hope. People who are in bondage to anxiety may not think they have much to be thankful for. If that's the case, let me suggest a place to start:

> "Dear Lord, I thank You that even though I am worried about what's happening, You have promised not to give me more than I can bear. Thank You for the times You have delivered me and answered prayer in the past, and for Your promise never to leave or forsake me. Thank You that I can cast all my anxieties on You, as 1 Peter 5:7 says, because I know You care for me. And even though I can't see any solution to my problem right now, I want to thank You for being more concerned about my needs than I am. Help me to trust You completely in this situation. Amen."

Now I need to warn you about something. If you start to pray with thanksgiving, it will be impossible to focus on your problem for very long. It will be impossible for worry to eat out your stomach lining when you are thanking God for His goodness, grace, and never-failing promises. Instead, you'll be filled with hope as you realize you are coming to a God who is "the same yesterday and today and forever" (Hebrews 13:8 NIV).

PRAYER BRINGS GOD'S PEACE

There's another benefit to praying about everything with fervent supplication and overflowing thanksgiving.

Paul described it in Philippians 4:7, where we read, "And the peace of God, *which surpasses all comprehension,* will guard your hearts and your minds in Christ Jesus" (emphasis added).

Peace is the opposite of turmoil and worry. Most people think peace requires the absence of problems, which seems to make sense. But not for God's people. That's why I emphasized the words above. God's peace doesn't make sense to the natural mind because it comes in the middle of our problems and in spite of our problems.

That's how you know that what you are experiencing is God's peace. It's peace that doesn't make sense, peace you can't conjure up on your own or manipulate. God's peace is when the storm hasn't died down, and yet you are singing. You are sleeping for the first time in weeks. Everything around you says you should be tearing your hair out, but you have a calmness of spirit that can't be explained apart from God.

Paul explained how this happens. The peace of God "will guard your hearts and your minds in Christ Jesus." This reminds me of a sentry on duty on the wall of a city. A sentry's job is to challenge anyone who wants to enter the city and only allow the right people in. God's peace stands guard at the gate of your mind and shuts it against worry. And this sentry is on duty 24/7, as the kids say.

When you look in the Bible for examples of God's peace, what you find are people who had it even in the most difficult circumstances. What about Daniel in the lions' den (Daniel 6:12–28), or Paul and Silas bleeding in prison at Philippi (Acts 16:23–25)? The king who tossed Daniel in the den couldn't sleep that night, but Daniel used the lions for a pillow. Paul and Silas held a praise service—and God delivered them.

That's why Paul could say, "Rejoice in the Lord always; again I will say, rejoice" (Philippians 4:4). He knew what he was talking about. Paul didn't write that as he sat in a café on the Mediterranean, sipping a cappuccino. He was under arrest and waiting to find out if he was going to released or executed.

MAKE YOURSELF A WORRY BOX

If you are prone to being anxious about things, I want you to make yourself a worry box. Take a shoe box or something and cut a hole in the lid. Then when Satan starts pushing you to worry, write down your concern, look up to God, and pray, "Lord, this is what I'm worried about. But You told me not to worry, so I am going to put this worry in my box as an admission that I can't handle it. This means it's Yours to handle, and I'm trusting You to take care of it."

Am I telling you all your problems will go away if you put them in a worry box? No, but I am telling you that when you learn to replace worry with prayer and faith, God will open an umbrella over you in the midst of your storm to keep you from getting drenched. And He will give you peace that surpasses all comprehension.

3

THE BLAST
OF
LIFE'S
STORMS

A few years ago my wife and I were on a cruise to Alaska with friends from our national ministry, The Urban Alternative. We were having a great time, but at one point our ship ran into a storm that quickly became scary.

Things got so turbulent that my wife called the captain and chided him for not knowing that there was such a frightening storm ahead of us. But the captain assured her that he knew the storm was out there and that we would be fine.

When you're in a storm on the sea and the ship is tossing back and forth, I can assure you it makes all the difference in the world to know that the person in charge has the situation under control. It's important to know the same thing when the storms of life hit, because I can assure you they will.

In fact, without even knowing your circumstances I can say with confidence that you're either coming out of a storm, in one right now, or heading into one. Storms that can create fear and anxiety are a part of life, whether we are talking about marital storms, financial storms, health storms, or any other kind of problem you can name.

Jesus said, "In the world you have tribulation" (John 16:33). That's a statement of fact. The apostle Peter wrote to believers, "Beloved, do not be surprised at the fiery ordeal among you, which comes upon you for your testing, as though some strange thing were happening to you" (1 Peter 4:12). We shouldn't be surprised when problems arrive.

A storm at sea is a powerful illustration of the problems that come into our lives. Talk about something that causes fear and anxiety. Being on a storm-tossed sea can be a helpless feeling, and few things look more threatening than dark, turbulent water. Perhaps that's why Jesus sent His disciples out into the middle of a storm one night on the Sea of Galilee (Matthew 14:22–34). He had some powerful, life-changing lessons to teach them—lessons we need today for times when God sends a storm of pain, suffering, loss, or other trial into our lives.

OUR STORMS COME
FROM GOD'S HAND

Yes, you read that correctly. Our trials are from God's hand, whether He sends them directly or allows them to arise in the normal course of events. Storms come for different reasons, as we will see. We are going to look at the storm that hit the disciples in the middle of the Sea of Galilee and the lessons we can learn from it about trusting God in a storm. The next chapter deals with these lessons, but I want to set the stage here by showing you how Jesus arranged and orchestrated this event that looked to His disciples like it might be their last night on earth.

It's a great story as told in Matthew 14, and the preceding context is an important part of the drama. In verses 13–21, Jesus had just performed one of His greatest miracles, the feeding of the five thousand—the only miracle repeated in all four gospels, by the way. So this must have been a magnificent, mind-boggling occasion for the disciples, especially considering the fact that the number *five thousand* just counted the men in the crowd. With the women and children added in, some estimates say that Jesus may have fed between fifteen and twenty thousand people.

Now we want to pick up what happened next, written in Matthew 14:22. The Bible says, "Immediately He made the disciples get into the boat and go ahead of Him to the other side, while He sent the crowds away."

Jesus followed this shining moment of blessing by sending the disciples into what would be a major storm.

Why did Jesus do that? Why does God send storms into our lives? We'll try to provide some answers as we go along, but I want you to see that Jesus brought both the blessing of the miracle and the blast of the storm. And both are part of life.

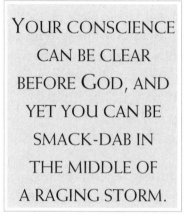

YOUR CONSCIENCE CAN BE CLEAR BEFORE GOD, AND YET YOU CAN BE SMACK-DAB IN THE MIDDLE OF A RAGING STORM.

Now a lot of Christians have a problem accepting the fact that God sends or allows storms to come, especially when they are trying to do His will and please Him. But if we believe that God is sovereign, and the Bible teaches from beginning to end that He is, that means He can do whatever is best to Him. And His love assures us that whatever He sends is for our good.

The disciples' situation in this story is a good example of what I'm talking about. They were in God's will when they hit this storm. Jesus told them to get into the boat and head to the other side of the sea, and they obeyed Him.

STORMS COME EVEN
WHEN WE ARE OBEYING GOD

Just because you're in a storm, don't assume that God is angry with you or has abandoned you. In fact, your storm may come precisely because you are seeking to obey God. This world is full of folk who get upset when Christians are faithful and obedient to God, and they will continue to make trouble for God's people. What I'm saying is that your conscience can be clear before God, and yet you can be smack-dab in the middle of a raging storm.

Of course, there are those storms that come when we are out of God's will and running from what He wants us to do. The rebellious prophet Jonah comes to mind. He didn't want to go to Nineveh and warn the people to repent, because he was afraid they would do so and be spared by God. Jonah didn't like that idea because the people of Nineveh, the capital of Assyria, were Israel's enemies. So Jonah ran the other way, but God tracked him down with a literal storm much like the one the disciples faced on the Sea of Galilee.

So the storms will come no matter what—but I'd much rather be in a storm within God's will than outside of it!

Returning to the story of the disciples whom Jesus sent out in a boat . . . After they set out, Jesus left and went up to a mountain to pray (Matthew 14:23). But in the meantime, things were getting rough on the sea.

"The boat was already a long distance from the land, battered by the waves; for the wind was contrary" (v. 24).

Contrary is a picturesque word. Ever had a child be contrary? We talk about mules being contrary too. It's the idea of someone or something resisting you and pulling against you no matter what you try to do. And usually, the harder you pull in one direction, the fiercer the resistance from the other side.

This was a fierce wind. And in his account of this story, Mark added that the disciples were "straining at the oars" (Mark 6:48). They were trying to row themselves out of the storm, but the harder they rowed, the harder the wind worked against them. In other words, they weren't making any progress.

When you're in a situation like this, you have to conclude that this is a divine appointment—a storm God wants you to be in for a while. If He didn't, He would let you row out of it pretty quickly. It's one thing to recognize that storms are inevitable as long as we live in a fallen, imperfect world. But it's another thing entirely to realize that there may be no quick exit from the fierce wind and turbulent water that are rocking your boat and threatening to capsize it.

Some years ago, a friend of mine went to the dentist with a sudden, painful toothache and heard the dreaded words, "You need a root canal." The dentist started in, and after working a while started putting his tools away and cleaning up. My friend said to him, "Well, that wasn't so bad."

"Oh, we've just done part of it," the dentist answered. And that's when my friend learned that he would have to return for "part two" of the procedure—and the second half of the process would be a lot more painful than the first.

That's the way life's storms often work. Most of us will readily admit that trials and problems are a part of life. But many of us start to panic during those times when the water is coming *into* the boat as well as against the boat, and it looks like we're going under. In these moments, fear and anxiety can well up and choke off our air.

I said that some Christians don't believe that severe storms can be God's will for His children, especially when they are doing His will. But the story we've been looking at directly contradicts that idea. We know the disciples' predicament was of divine origin because Jesus sent them directly into the storm. The writer of Hebrews said, "Those whom the Lord loveth He spanketh" (Hebrews 12:6, my paraphrase).

Where Is God in Our Storms?

For us as Christians, this is the real question we are asking, whether we say it out loud or not. We read above that after sending the disciples out onto the Sea of Galilee and into a storm He knew was coming, Jesus stayed behind to pray.

The easiest thing in the world is to feel forgotten by

God when you're struggling with a serious problem and fear has a grip on your heart and mind. I know from years of pastoral counseling that many Christians in these situations wish God would send them some sort of sign, or even show up and tell them what He is doing and why. The title of a best-selling book written a few years ago addressed the question many people ask during a storm: *Where Is God When It Hurts?*

Well, we know for sure where Jesus was on this occasion in Matthew 14. He was praying on a mountain—and I believe He was praying for the disciples, that their faith would not fail. More on that kind of faith in the concluding chapter.

Let me ask you a question. Do you think it would have been a different story that night if Jesus had gone with the disciples to be there when the blast of the storm hit?

This is a trick question, because I know the answer. Jesus *was* with the apostles one night during a different storm. According to Mark 4:35–41, they were crossing the sea when struck by "a fierce gale of wind." Jesus was right there in the boat, asleep on a cushion in the back, and yet the disciples still panicked. They even accused Jesus: "Teacher, do You not care that we are perishing?" (v. 38). And in this case, too, just as He did in Matthew 14, Jesus had to rebuke them for having little or no faith.

What I'm saying is that even if God were to write in the sky, "I am with you; do not be afraid," our human tendency would still be to give in to fear and anxiety during a tough trial. But it's precisely at those times that our faith needs to be at its strongest, or it really isn't worth much. Anybody can believe when the job is solid, the bank account is full, the kids are making you proud, and the doctor can't find anything wrong with you.

So where is God in our storms? He's right there beside us in the darkness, even when we don't sense His presence. As we mentioned earlier, He has promised never to leave or forsake us (Hebrews 13:5). But because we are humans, we like to have someone we can see and touch when we feel alone in the dark. We're like the little girl who was crying in her room one night and calling for her mother.

Mom went in and asked what was wrong. "I'm scared to be alone in the dark," the girl said.

"But, honey, you don't have to be afraid. Remember, Jesus is with you."

"I know, Mommy," the girl said, "but I need someone with skin on."

JESUS KNOWS WHEN TO SHOW UP

Please don't misunderstand this statement. We just said that God is always with us in our storms. But He has also promised to give us special grace for trials, as He said to Paul: "My grace is sufficient for you" (2 Corinthians 12:9).

That's why I say Jesus will come to you in your trial when the time is right. However, His time may not be

your time. We read in Matthew 14:24 that the disciples'
boat was "a long distance from the land" before Jesus left
the mountain. Peter and his pals were rowing for all they
were worth but not getting anywhere and getting more
scared by the minute.

Why did Jesus let the Twelve get into that mess?
One reason was to teach them that human ability alone
is not enough to get us through life's storms. Why does
God send storms your way? For the same reason. God
wants you to discover that when you hit rock bottom,
He is the rock at the bottom!

JESUS WILL SEND THE
NEXT STORM AT THE RIGHT TIME

You say, "Tony, I could have done without this point.
I was hoping there would be an easier way to learn the
lesson." Well, my experience tells me that most of us
don't really begin to learn life's most important lessons
until we have been put to the test. And most of us need
more than one pass to get the message.

Let's suppose Jesus had held a "mini-Bible confer-
ence" there at the seaside before sending the disciples
out into the boat. Suppose He wrote on a blackboard
numerous references from the Old Testament that speak
of God's care for His people during times of trouble and
had the disciples record these passages in their confer-
ence notebooks and memorize them. Then suppose He
called for testimonies of times when God had sustained

these men in hard times, led them in a rousing hymn of faith, and sent them out. Do you think they would have breezed right through that storm?

I don't think so, for a very simple reason. We are slow learners. There is biblical evidence for that in this story. Mark's account says that when Jesus got into the boat and the storm stopped, the disciples were amazed—not out of faith, but out of unbelief, "for they had not gained any insight from the incident of the loaves, but their heart was hardened" (Mark 6:52).

WE HAVE TO FACE THE TRUTH THAT STORMS ARE A GOD-ORDAINED PART OF LIFE.

It takes time and repeated experience to learn life's lessons, and there are usually some scrapes, bruises, and even scars in the process.

Dad, when your four-year-old fell and scraped her knee that first time learning to ride her bicycle, did you immediately sell the bike and assure her that that nasty old thing would never hurt her again?

I hope not. Why? Because smart parents know they can't shield their kids from all of life's bumps, and they don't want to. Parents who don't allow their four-year-old to ride a bike or play outdoors for fear she might get a scrape or a bruise, or don't help her know what it's like to fall and get up again and get back on the bike, are setting her up to be one terribly dependent, fearful twenty-four-year-old someday.

Now when his child falls and scrapes her knee, a loving father is certainly going to scoop her up in his arms, carry her into the house to treat the wound, and hold her close while she cries. That's what God does for us in our pain. But a wise father will also encourage his child to go back out and try it again, because that's the only way to learn to ride a bike.

So we have to face the truth that storms are a God-ordained part of life. They are inevitable, and they can be intense and even incapacitating for a time.

But here's the good news. There's a blessing behind the blast of each storm that hits, and you can find it by learning to trust God in the middle of your storms. Let's talk about it.

4

THE BLESSING
IN
LIFE'S
STORMS

One of the most dramatic pieces of film ever recorded was made in the late 1930s. It documented the attempt of a German dirigible, or airship, to land at a naval field in America after crossing the Atlantic.

The ship dropped a number of long ropes down to sailors on the ground, who were waiting to grab them and tie the ship down. But just as the sailors took hold of the ropes, a gust of wind swept the ship back up into the air, pulling several sailors with it.

Two of the terrified sailors hung on desperately to the same rope, one above the other, their white navy scarves flapping in the wind as they rose into the air. They were afraid to let go of the rope, even though they were being lifted higher and higher. Finally, the film recorded the tragedy of these two sailors being pulled over a thousand feet into the air, where first one and then the other lost his grip and plunged to his death.

Even though most of the storms we face are not life-and-death situations, we know what it feels like to be holding on to the small end of a big problem as we are swept along helplessly by the situation. We know that if we keep clinging to our fear we'll just get into more trouble, but we're too afraid to let go.

That's where Jesus' disciples were in Matthew 14 as they battled fear and anxiety, along with huge waves and "contrary" winds, while fearing for their lives on the Sea of Galilee one terrifying night (v. 24). These conditions don't sound like the ingredients for a blessing, but I want to pick up the story again and show you that God had something good for the disciples despite the storm.

We have already mentioned a key element of this story, which is that the storm hit the disciples while they were in God's will. Jesus had told them to get into the boat and go to the other side, so the disciples were in the right place at the right time.

I hope you don't believe that hard times aren't supposed to come to God's people when we are doing what He wants us to do. If someone told you that, I would like to correct the misinformation. Storms come, period. God uses life's setbacks and challenges to perfect and mature us, so you can be sure He doesn't waste His storms or send them randomly.

But the storms will come. The only question is

when, what their intensity will be, and what our reaction will be.

Of course, not every trial we face comes in the middle of doing right. Remember Jonah. God often sends a storm to track us down and turn us around. You may ask, "How will I know the difference?"

Trust me, God often shows us the reasons behind pain. Even a small child knows the difference between getting a spanking when he disobeys and getting a shot at the doctor's when a virus is going around in his school.

> THERE IS NO CIRCUMSTANCE YOU HAVE FACED THAT CHRIST IS NOT ACUTELY FAMILIAR WITH.

Jesus deliberately placed the disciples in a storm—but let me tell you something exciting. They were fine because God was with them and was watching over them, as we will see. You are safer in a storm in God's will than you are on dry ground outside of God's will. So let me share some of the blessings that people discover in the midst of their storms.

JESUS IS PRAYING FOR YOU

You'll recall that after Jesus sent the disciples away in the boat, He stayed behind on a mountain to pray (Matthew 14:23). This raises a question. What relationship did Jesus' praying have to the disciples' rough

sailing? The Bible says that Jesus Christ "always lives to
make intercession for [believers]" (Hebrews 7:25). That
means even when you are not praying for yourself, Jesus
is praying for you.

It's important to know Jesus is praying for you. He
understands where you're coming from. There is no cir-
cumstance you have faced that Christ is not acutely fa-
miliar with.

What might Jesus have been praying for on the
mountain that night? I know one thing Jesus prayed for
Peter, because His words are recorded in Luke
22:31–32: "Simon, Simon, behold, Satan has demanded
permission to sift you like wheat; but I have prayed for
you, that your faith may not fail; and you, when once
you have turned again, strengthen your brothers."

Now I know that this was what Jesus said to Peter
the night he betrayed the Lord. But Peter's faith would
also be on trial on this night in Matthew 14, and Peter
needed Jesus' intercession even though he didn't know
he needed it.

Peter wasn't the only person Jesus prayed for in a
storm. He's praying for you today, because He is alive forever. When Jesus prays for you in your storm, it's that
your faith might remain strong in spite of the circumstances you are in. He is praying for the development of
your faith, because that's what all of our trials are designed
to do—even those that arise from our disobedience.

So when storms are splashing water all over you,
know that God is up to something. He wants to develop

your faith, to expand your trust and knowledge of Him. And remember, Jesus feels what you feel. Hebrews 4:15 says that Jesus is a sympathetic high priest who identifies with us in our trials. He is praying for you by name, and with the heart of a caring Father!

JESUS WILL COME
TO YOU AT THE RIGHT TIME

We touched on this point in the previous chapter, but I want to develop it here. The Bible says that Jesus came to the disciples on the Sea of Galilee "in the fourth watch of the night" (Matthew 14:25). That's between three and six o'clock in the morning, when normal folk are sleeping.

But the disciples were not asleep at that hour, and neither are many of us when we're battling a severe emotional storm. David said, "I am weary with my sighing; every night I make my bed swim, I dissolve my couch with my tears" (Psalm 6:6). Can you identify? Praise God that Jesus comes to you even in the wee hours of the morning. David knew that and also wrote, "When I remember You on my bed, I meditate on You in the night watches" (Psalm 63:6).

But Jesus didn't come to the disciples until it was dark, they were a long distance from the shore, and their peace of mind had been totally disrupted. Why did He wait so long? For the same reason wise and loving parents don't try to run ahead of their children and clear away all the obstacles so they never have to deal with life's bumps, disagreeable people, or the consequences of their own mistakes and sins.

If God bailed us out of every storm while we were still in shallow water, we'd never learn anything worthwhile about His power or promises.

JESUS WILL ADDRESS THE REAL ISSUE

Jesus waited until the disciples were in a mess, and when He arrived He didn't fix the problem right away. Or did He?

A person's viewpoint is seldom the same as God's view. The disciples thought their only problem was the storm that was rocking their boat. But instead of calming the waves and wind and then talking to His men, Jesus came to them walking on top of the problem. He didn't change the circumstances right away. In fact, the only thing that changed was that Jesus was now with them in their dilemma. Just as God promised in Isaiah 43:2: "When you pass through the waters, I [the Lord] will be with you."

The way God deals with us in our storms often throws us into confusion. The first thing we would expect Jesus to do is to calm the storm. After all, how could the disciples focus on what the Lord was trying to teach them when they were so afraid and distracted?

That's a good question—but it's the wrong question. It is precisely in those times when the wind and waves are roaring the loudest that God wants us to look for and listen to Him.

Let me throw you a curveball here. In Mark's account of this same storm, he added an interesting detail. Jesus not only came to the disciples in the middle of the sea, but "He intended to pass by them" (Mark 6:48). Jesus saw them straining at the oars and putting forth all the effort they could to make some progress. But He acted like He was going to walk right on by them.

What was going on here? There is a lesson that we need today. If you are determined to try and solve your problems by grunting and groaning, huffing and puffing on your own, God will let you do that until you are ready to cry out to Him for help. When we put Mark 6 with Matthew 14, we understand that one reason Peter cried out to Jesus is that it looked to him like Jesus was going to pass them by.

It's wonderful to have Jesus show up in your storm. Just be prepared to talk about the real deal when He comes. Now don't misunderstand. Jesus cares about your trial. During another storm on the sea, Jesus was asleep in the back of the boat when the disciples shook Him awake with this question: "Teacher, do You not care that we are perishing?" (Mark 4:38).

Of course Jesus cared. He got up and stopped the storm. But instead of speaking soothing words about how much He loved them, He rebuked them for their accusation: "Why are you so afraid? Do you still have no faith?" (v. 40 NIV).

Most of us treat God the way we do our doctors. We go to the doc when we're hurting, looking for a fix for the pain. But the doctor also wants to talk to us about our lack of exercise, bad eating habits, high blood pressure or cholesterol, or other underlying issues that may be contributing to or even causing the pain.

Jesus cares about your storm—but He cares about *you* more. And His first priority is to strengthen your faith and deepen your trust in Him so that when the next storm hits, you won't have to strain so hard trying to fix the mess yourself. Jesus knew the real issue that night was the need of the disciples (particularly Peter) to learn several important lessons.

First, they needed a new revelation of Jesus' power. You won't seek Jesus until you really believe He can do something about your storm.

Second, the disciples needed to learn that they had a choice, just as we have. We can grunt and groan ourselves while Jesus walks right past us, or we can give up the fight and call out to Him. That's why Jesus acted as if He intended to keep on walking past them.

Third, the disciples needed greater faith in Him. They needed to understand that Jesus did not send them out to the middle of the sea to drown but to get to the other side. They needed to learn there is no reason for fear when Jesus shows up.

So the real issue in your storm is not necessarily the severity of it or your desire to get away from it. The question is, are you going to keep straining to fix it yourself and let Jesus pass you by, or are you going to call on Him to do what you can't do? Some of us have been straining for years to fix the problems in our lives, but the harder we try, the worse the problems get. Ultimately, the only solution is to call on God.

LOOK FOR JESUS IN YOUR STORM

The Bible says, "When the disciples saw [Jesus] walking on the sea, they were terrified, and said, 'It is a ghost!' And they cried out in fear" (Matthew 14:26).

Why didn't the disciples recognize Jesus? Because they weren't looking for Him. Do you know how many times Jesus has passed you by? If you're not looking for Him, you're not going to see Him. He could be right by your boat.

Fear and anxiety negate faith and keep you from seeing Jesus when He comes to you in your trial. Whenever something happens in your life that makes you afraid, that fear is a call to faith. The moment you feel fearful and anxious, you have just heard God say, "Look to Me."

When you pray, "Lord, I'm afraid right now because the winds of my circumstances are against me. But I will trust You, right now," that's when you will hear Him say, "Take courage, it is I; do not be afraid" (Matthew 14:27). I don't know what God is going to say to you about your storm, but I do know He is going to say, "I am here."

Like my Hebrew boys Shadrach, Meshach, and Abednego in Daniel 3, you may be in the fiery furnace, but you won't be there alone. Even while you're waiting for God to change the storm on the outside, go to God to take care of the storm on the inside. You can go a long way just knowing He is there.

KEEP YOUR EYES ON JESUS

When Peter saw Jesus coming toward the boat, he spoke up and said, "Lord, if it is You, command me to come to You on the water" (Matthew 14:28). Peter was ready to try anything, but he was no dummy. He decided he was better off with Jesus on the stormy water than he was hanging out in the boat with his "homeys." Jesus was getting somewhere, while the disciples were stuck.

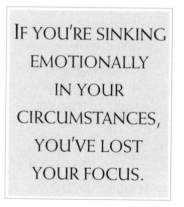

IF YOU'RE SINKING EMOTIONALLY IN YOUR CIRCUMSTANCES, YOU'VE LOST YOUR FOCUS.

Too many of us hang with folk who are going nowhere—talking a good game and bragging about what they've done, when the truth is they're struggling as much as we are.

Peter had the right idea when he told Jesus he wanted to join Him. So Jesus told Peter to step out, and as long as Peter kept his eyes on Jesus, he walked on that stormy, thrashing water. What would it be like if your faith in Christ grew so strong that even when your circumstances didn't change, you were walking on top of them with Jesus instead of being under them?

But soon Peter took his eyes off the Person he was walking toward and started focusing on the water he was walking on. That's when he started to sink.

If you're sinking emotionally in your circumstances, you've lost your focus. You're paying your storm too much attention. I know you can't ignore the storm. Jesus didn't ask Peter to do that but to take Him at His word and walk to Him. Jesus was teaching Peter to trade self-sufficiency for Christ-sufficiency. Peter got the message when he cried out, "Lord, save me!" (v. 30).

You may say, "Tony, I'm sinking in my storm, but the Lord isn't saving me." Maybe it's because you're circumstantially driven. If so, you need to refocus your spiritual eyes on Jesus, as the author of Hebrews tells us to "[fix] our eyes on Jesus" (Hebrews 12:2).

JESUS WILL REWARD YOUR FAITH

I love what happened to Peter next. "Immediately Jesus stretched out His hand and took hold of him, and said to him, 'You of little faith, why did you doubt?'" (v. 31). The word *doubt* has the idea of wavering back and forth, being "double-minded" (James 1:8). Peter was trying to focus on Jesus and his circumstances at the same time.

It took great faith for Peter to step out of the boat, but he went from great faith to little faith in a short time. It's possible to go from great faith to little faith when we take our eyes off Jesus. But praise the Lord—it is also possible to go from little faith to great faith when we believe Him. And God will not overlook even little faith, although it should never be our goal to stay in that condition.

Why did Jesus tell Peter he had little faith? Because of that one word Jesus had spoken: "Come." In other words, Jesus was not going to let Peter drown halfway to Him, just as He didn't send the disciples out onto the lake to die in a storm. Anything Jesus starts, He finishes.

Hebrews 12:2 adds this wonderful truth about Jesus: He is "the author and perfecter of faith." Earlier the writer had said that it is impossible to please God without faith, but that He is "a rewarder of those who seek Him" (Hebrews 11:6).

God wants to develop your faith through trials, and He rewards you for acting in faith. Peter learned that lesson well. Many years later, he wrote these words to believers undergoing a fierce storm of persecution: "Now for a little while, if necessary, you have been distressed by various trials, so that the proof of your faith, being more precious than gold which is perishable, even though tested by fire, may be found to result in praise and glory and honor at the revelation of Jesus Christ" (1 Peter 1:6–7).

Matthew 14:32 says that when Jesus got into the boat, the storm stopped. The storm didn't cease until Jesus had made His point. Your storm is not going to stop until you stop rowing, until you let go of your fear and anxiety and invite Jesus into your boat.

John's version of this story adds another interesting detail. When Jesus got into the boat and the storm stopped, they were "immediately" at their destination on the other side of the sea (John 6:21). Here's the reward for faith. Once you get your eyes on Jesus and begin trusting Him, you get where you're going a lot faster than you would if you tried to row yourself there. Jesus can take you immediately to places you have been straining to reach for years.

Matthew concludes: "Those who were in the boat worshiped Him, saying, 'You are certainly God's Son!'" (v. 33). If you wonder whether Jesus can replace your fear and anxiety with peace, and help you walk on top of your circumstances, you need a storm because it will give you something to walk on. Let go of the oars and invite Jesus into your boat, and you'll get where you wanted to go all the time.

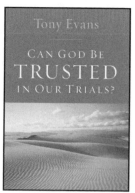

LET IT GO! TEAM

ACQUIRING EDITOR
Greg Thornton

COPY EDITOR
Ali Childers

BACK COVER COPY
Lauren Lintner

COVER DESIGN
Smartt Guys

COVER PHOTO
Dandelion: Steve Cole/Getty Images

INTERIOR DESIGN
Ragont Design

PRINTING AND BINDING
Versa Press, Inc.

The typeface for the text of this book is
Weiss